PRICED OUT

OTHER TITLES FROM THE EMMA PRESS

POETRY PAMPHLETS

Paisley, by Rakhshan Rizwan
Elastic Glue, by Kathy Pimlott
Dear Friend(s), by Jeffery Sugarman
Poacher, by Lenni Sanders

SHORT STORIES

First fox, by Leanne Radojkovich
Postcard Stories, by Jan Carson
The Secret Box, by Daina Tabūna
Once Upon A Time In Birmingham, by Louise Palfreyman

POETRY ANTHOLOGIES

Some Cannot Be Caught: The Emma Press Book of Beasts
In Transit: Poems of Travel
Second Place Rosette: Poems about Britain
Everything That Can Happen: Poems about the Future

BOOKS FOR CHILDREN

The Dog Who Found Sorrow, by Rūta Briede
The Head that Wears a Crown: Poems about Kings and Queens
The Girl Who Learned All the Languages Of The World,
by Ieva Flamingo
Wain, by Rachel Plummer
The Adventures of Na Willa, by Reda Gaudiamo

POETRY AND ART SQUARES

AWOL, by John Fuller and Andrew Wynn Owen
Now You Can Look, by Julia Bird, illustrated by Anna Vaivare
The Goldfish, by Ikhda Ayuning Maharsi Degoul,
illustrated by Emma Wright

PRICED OUT

By Conor Cleary

WITH AN INTRODUCTION BY
LUKE KENNARD

THE EMMA PRESS

First published in the UK in 2019 by the Emma Press Ltd

Poems copyright © Conor Cleary 2019
Introduction copyright © Luke Kennard 2019

All rights reserved.

The right of Conor Cleary to be identified as the author of this work has been asserted in accordance with the Copyright, Designs and Patents Act 1988.

Edited by Richard O'Brien
Typeset by Emma Wright

ISBN 978-1-912915-25-5

A CIP catalogue record of this book is available from the British Library.

The Emma Press
theemmapress.com
hello@theemmapress.com
Birmingham, UK

INTRODUCTION

What do we read for when encountering a new voice for the first time? For some refreshing or distinctive sense of language, sure, and for form. In the case of this pamphlet we'd find a facility for excising punctuation when it counts to rival W. S. Merwin's tragi-comic timing and masterful use of line-break; not to mention a bravura final sonnet sequence as accomplished as it is natural. But mostly we read for the same reason we always go to poetry: for some consolation, some insight into how we account for it all, in spite of feeling ill-at-ease or somehow inadequate most of the time.

priced out simmers with the quiet anger of engagement, leavened with a wise and enviably broad imagination. Where the narrator might metamorphose into a less than appetising dessert or, in the plaintive but astute love-song of 'webbing' (page 9), a terrifying mechanical spider. We want to be seen and loved for who we are, but what are we hiding and what if it's awful? And what if we're worthy of love anyway?

There is such assurance here, even at its most self-lacerating, and a reminder that we all have to find "a way of fixating on the world's finer instances". Ultimately I read for a poet who can look outwards as fearlessly as they look inwards, and this collection is endlessly curious in its segues into ancient and recent, art and personal history, because we are what we love.

All of this is done with such a deceptive lightness of touch; Cleary can find meaning in the arcane history of bees or the touchingly aspirational house names in a dreary suburb and then break your heart with a description of intimacy as brief and precise as a meaningful look. It's beautiful – and to be honest I'd rather you hadn't read this first, that you'd just skipped directly to the poems, but I suppose it's too late for that now and I can only offer my apologies.

Luke Kennard
APRIL 2019

CONTENTS

Meditations on a Vine; or, I am the Sand Guardian, Guardian of the Sand 1
Exchange 3
piña 4
oviedo 5
errata: in six tweets 6
collision 8
webbing 9
The Mousse 11
real tree 12
Tell 13
wild divine 15
Roots 16

priced out
prologue: to my mother at my age 17
1 18
2 19
3 20
4 21
5 22
6 23
7 24
8 25
9 26

Acknowledgements 27
About the poet 28
About the Emma Press 28

Meditations on a Vine; or, I am the Sand Guardian, Guardian of the Sand

I mean, we're all looking for something to buy into. Tell me you're some kind of Guardian, or on a Quest, or that the Kingdom depends on your doing X or Y, and I'll buy it every time, hook, line and sinker. I have an overactive appetite when it comes to wanting to believe in things. I've wanted to believe in toothpaste and car insurance; I've wanted to believe in most things you see on TV. I've even wanted to believe in the economy and that on average we all more or less get what's coming to us.

And so, when the guy on screen manages to fit so much conviction into so small a phrase, I'm already taking his word for it. That kind of rhetoric is hard to come by, these days. It reminds me of the books I used to read as a teenager, with knights and lords and castles. I would fall asleep almost every night imagining myself surrounded by battlements and impregnable walls.

By the time Poseidon is insulted, I'm picturing an ancient, never-ending feud between the sea and the shore; the Sand Guardian and the God of the Ocean. This is the kind of story I can get my head around. Elemental. Instinctual. Played out over and over again in primary colours. It's huge and it's exaggerated like Lex Luthor vs. Superman or Sauron vs. Frodo or my desire to get up early and work hard vs. my desire to stay in bed all day and masturbate.

It's easy to empathize with someone shouting at the tide and at some point or another, everyone's diction burns away and like a sauce is reduced to a single, viscous *fuck off*.

I'm sure if I wanted, I could want to believe in sand. There's something encouraging about the way a beach will follow you home, inside your shoes and under your fingernails; and I like the idea of something like a god I can pack into a bucket and make castles out of. And no, sandcastles are not impregnable, or even insoluble, and yes, there is a sense in which a sandcastle is the exact opposite of a castle. But I mean, we're all looking for something to buy into, and you can say what you want about sand, but you can't say it's hard to come by.

Exchange

I have a medievalist's obsession with luxury resources.
Citrus, glass and cane sugar: Europe's great absences

during the Dark Ages. I love the clock in *Faustus*
as the Modern Age shudders in. I love the atlas

that shows California as an island
and the other over-wide lands soon to be pared down by sciences.

But more than rivers of silver driven from
La Plata to Cádiz and Christendom,

more than more Habsburg coinage
or westward Atlantic voyages

my medieval tongue marvels
at the compacting of gradual handfuls

and handfuls
of young coffee seeds into instant coffee granules.

piña

after Oviedo's sketch of a pineapple

of course there will be botanists
ripe with pride on their knees in front of monarchs
across the whole of this temperate continent

there will be hothouses and pineries
and the sheer graft and inconvenience
of forcing you to flower at these latitudes

you'll find yourself as centrepiece
unsliced uneaten recycled for dinner parties
until you begin rotting from the core

and once in the mind of the nobility
the idea of you has been firmly established
as something prestigious and expensive

you'll be abstracted further still
from your flesh and juices and fashioned
into stone bollards along grand driveways

but for now before any of this
you are a drawing of an armoured thing
risen out of sierras half a globe away

you are as close to mythological
as the modern world can allow for
with potential inside you for hatching dragons

oviedo

da vinci no less praised his silhouettes
called him according to some sources
a veritable god with a pair of scissors

from a single sheet of unruled paper
he could cut almost any profile you named
a face a figure the entire city of milan

to the delight of lords and ladies
he would negotiate with fingers and thumbs
the edges of the page under itself

form improbable series of triangles
in a careful array of ratios
held together by seams and surface friction

he would pack it down into his palm
until it looked like a mistake
like he had backed himself into a corner

and just as it seemed
you were a fool to believe it possible
and the whole project a failure

out would come the scissors in a flurry
and all the excess would fall away
leaving behind the startling likeness

of a habsburg or a dolphin
domes towers and bunting
the white shadow of a new century

errata: in six tweets

for Fionn

apart from general chit-chat
he had some beautiful tweets:
manuscript illuminations & vellum
codices with dead alphabets
& gilded marginalia

he did a series on medieval bees
& medieval attitudes to bees;
how people thought
they were tiny fuzzy birds
that built castles & kept kings

he had pictures of hunched merchants
capturing bees in sacks,
their clothes impractical
& two-dimensional & dyed
a near-perfect vibrant blue

he said blue was the most expensive colour
because the trade routes
needed to import indigo
had not been invented yet:
this was lapis lazuli

another had bees with too many legs
& too many wings.
he said this was aristotle's fault
because he wrote about it
& never bothered to count

one had thatched beehives
& bees the size of roosters.
one had a farmer approaching the bees
with a sickle in hand
which I thought was brave

collision

when we bumble
into one another
on your couch

in the middle
of some dumb
semaphorical waltz

we let out
a little *whoop*
like polite arthropods

webbing

for Toby

what would you say
if it turned out
i was a giant
mechanical
spider who
didn't really
like the things we
both said we liked

if on further
inspection you
were to discover
my insides were
chock-full of
counterfeit silk
and i hated
your friend lisa

what if my gums
concealed big steel
fangs needed to eat
that retracted
seamlessly
that envenomed
that were very
much part of me

i hope that you'd
take a step back
think rationally
try to see things
as seen from
my perspective
hung upside down
from the ceiling

The Mousse

I feel particularly
gelatinous in Madrid
where it's easy to imagine
I'm some sort of awful
foreign dessert:

translucent and milky, still
wobbling after the waiter
deposits me on the table
in front of you. Did you
make a mistake

ordering from the Spanish
menu? Maybe you thought
you were getting the mousse?
Had you hoped for something
different entirely?

Please, don't be embarrassed.
We've all been guilty,
on occasion, of leaving something
behind us on the plate.
I have a thick skin.

It's hardly appetising.
And given the choice, *à la carte*,
I'm not exactly what I'd go for
myself. Not even my own
cup of tea.

If I am referenced at all
in the guidebooks to the city,
it is as an *acquired taste*
or, perhaps at a stretch,
a delicacy.

real tree

my nana told me how my aunt
got allergies one year suddenly
from the christmas tree

how she took steroids for a week
to no avail in hopes of keeping
a real tree in her living room

she had to give up at 3am
on the 24th when it came down
to authenticity or breathing

she slipped out to the supermarket
open all night for christmas
and got a flat-packed tree instead

i can't stop imagining her doing the swap
the silent undecorating
the indignant ornaments on the floor

temporarily
i can't stop being impressed
by this colossal sleight of hand

the next morning my aunt asked her family
if they noticed anything different
and her husband panicked and said she looked nice

it was almost new year's
when he took out the vacuum
and noticed there were no pine needles

Tell

On weekends, we come out to the orchard
to shoot at one another.
Our weapon of choice is the crossbow.

Today it's my turn at the trigger
so I get into costume:
Robin Hood jerkin, armoured skirt,

tights that flatter my calves.
Every inch of me is vegan green except
the crushed-insect red of my cap.

My boots have no orientation.
I alternate them from foot to foot
to make sure the heels are worn down evenly.

Your role requires ropes
and you shrug yourself into them
effortlessly, like Houdini in reverse.

Knots materialize out of nothing.
You find the friction between surfaces
and put it to work for you

and just like that, you're done, *voilà!*
tied up like a pork steak!
I finish you off with an apple

picked at random from the orchard floor.
It's massive, green and brown,
the kind only used for cooking.

I place it on your head like a crown.
You count out the paces for me
flirtatiously, and when you're far behind

I pivot on my perfectly level heels,
crank the bow into tension with itself,
take no particular aim, and fire.

wild divine

this old god only haunts heaths and hillsides and quaint places

he has been impoverished by cities

he missed his chance to carve out a new niche when he refused grooming

the ordnance survey dealt him a sore blow

his petty revenges range from bog drownings to muddied boots to death from exposure

all are more avoidable than he'd like

he's become less deliberate

his outbursts are more frequent and starting to worry his friends who keep urging him to talk to someone (which he refuses)

he is dirty from crawling under gorse bushes: keeping account of and hoarding their secrets

his spheres of influence are shrinking and rolling away

whatever he's holding down you couldn't call it a job

he refuses to get a car but is always borrowing his sister's

he gorges himself on fistfuls of robins

when you encounter his apparition it doesn't look like he's been eating

Roots

I

Houses that look like they might've looked good in the 80s:
despite my parents' denials, I suspect this used to be

a wealthier place. There's something vaguely Mediterranean
about the monkey puzzle trees and faux colonnades in

the fronts of houses with names. *Aisling View. Ave Maria.* One,
ambitiously, *Melbourne.*

II

My parents look beautiful in photographs from
the 80s: coral rose bouquet in hand, in lapel, beside them

a tiny marble statue of a couple; beside that an ashtray.
Imagine the hairstyles, the smoking indoors, the clay

and gravel of the hotel driveway and the wedding car on it.
Tin cans at the back, flowers on the bonnet.

III

Sometimes Tralee looks petrifying to me.
I'm scared by its greyness, its smallness and I see

its roads as runways.

priced out

prologue: to my mother at my age

while the bubble still glistens like a weekend away
and each year of the nineties sits on the calendar
in front of you like a fat promise
and both your parents are alive and around the corner

and in the papers and the magazines and on the weather
the threat of nuclear annihilation has subsided
to the point where you can start buying garden furniture
and speaking candidly to your doctor about sex

drive west to the fuchsia and the holiday homes
where on hot late nights you are implored
by friends and strangers alike to sing and sing and sing

because the icecaps are melting
and xtravision despite its robust complexion
will liquidate its stock and eventually cease trading

1

you've been learning how to want to stockpile
like a hoarder like a burning obsession
for newspapers jars of garlic peel old t-shirts
will keep you safe below the rampart

you wake up one day and realise you're overextended
like alexander the great without telling you
has been pushing your borders into india
against the better advice of his generals

your nerves can't handle any more smalltalk
or the year-long intervals between award ceremonies
wax wings don't offer the kind of contingencies you require

and the summer sky though pink and turquoise
and the kind of thing you used to lust after like a trophy
is crowded with demigods burning up on reentry

2

paranoid that your cousins have become successful
and the last four men who fucked you were medicis
and did so only thanks to a genetic predisposition
to want to patronize the arts

you begin keeping ledgers about the house
under the sink on the vanity table
you feed them every conceivable kind of receipt
until they are as fat and as purple as a bishop

this is what it takes to make you feel less naked
less like you've arrived at the counter of a shop
only to be told what you're carrying isn't legal tender

you are tired in your bones from scrutiny
you want clean white sheets and reassurances
access again to the cities you've been priced out of

3

to discourage your grandparents from travelling abroad
you invent a friend with salmonella
and detail in broad colour strokes the misery
of four nights spent vomiting in a hospital gown in greece

better by far the comforts of their own home
impervious to undercooked chicken or faulty atms
which at a moment's notice could swallow whole
your debit card and a lifetime's worth of savings

stay put you tell them and isn't killarney glorious
and only half a tank of petrol down the road
the county brims over with beauty this time of year

and if good health is a season to be savoured in full
is it not best spent amid familiar landscapes
encircled by those with your best interest at heart

4

because both your father and your grandfather
are award-winning studio photographers
and have between them five decades of experience
coaxing extended families into pleasing arrangements

you avoid making an amateur's mistake
and wear nothing more fashionable than required
you've seen too many instances of double denim
go eternally out of style on a living room wall

you suppose you have a kind of instinct for it
and fantasize occasionally about setting up shop
discovering that it all comes naturally

you know from osmosis the meaning of words
like exposure aperture saturation
you like the familiar shape they make of your mouth

5

your father you infer from a general sense of unease
and the consistency with which he skips meals
finds something unnerving about sitting down
to eat dinner at a table with other human beings

you read somewhere this implies a morbid denial
of one's own mortality and is not uncommon
among politicians careerists capricorns
and the eldest surviving child of a catholic household

once on holiday in portugal he was trapped
in a chinese with the rest of the family
and having wolfed down a cheeseburger in three bites

he informed you stephen hawking was a charlatan
whose only tangible contribution to physics
was the popularization of the phrase heat death

6

always eager for distraction on sunday nights
which from childhood have somehow managed to preserve
the slight sour unease of unfinished homework
you arrange laundry in piles according to urgency

in a half-hearted sort of way you want to return
to those analogue days when tvs fuzzed with static
and information was a thing that took fewer liberties
and could be shut up in a cartridge in a drawer

you are convinced you own fewer trousers than is typical
for a man your age especially a gay man
whose vocation often sees him in the public eye

you refer to both the washing machine and the dishwasher
as the washing machine which is technically correct
and have only ever used one setting on either

7

discovering to your complete surprise four am
and its strange extremes of temperature its night air
and open windows its sheets and blankets and bodies
that collide like weather fronts in sharp isothermic lines

and conceding that five consecutive nights
of the same person making you vulnerable
and teaching you facts about the space shuttle
need not be considered a vesuvian calamity

you allow yourself to be persuaded a little more
each time he tells you that the earth is flat
and the simplest proof of this is to view it from space

what good is a world after all without an edge
you can fall from and to paraphrase jfk
we do not do these things because they are safe

8

in bed watching documentaries about barnacle geese
whose young cascade themselves over slate cliff faces
because of evolution and sometimes despite this
if unlucky later in life are eaten by foxes

and films about singing aristocrats who decay
in their homes in the hamptons after the twenties
boom themselves out and whose gardens and accents
overgrow all sense of neighbourly propriety

he tells you he feels safe here and now
and that is like a warm tide rushing over you
and you apologise and cry and apologise

his dark eyes his hair his voice when exercised deliberately
are another shape of language altogether another
way of fixating on the world's finer instances

9

romantic impulses if films teach us anything
rarely go unpunished and so you are amazed
after stealing yourselves into the law building
and daring to push the button for the top floor

to be rewarded with an entire city
and the full clean panoramic of a september morning
its clarity waking you up like a coastline
like salt water in the air on your skin

and you both pick out a portion of belfast
according to greenery architecture mere whim
and like emperors in careless negotiation

swap church spires and bridges back and forth
exchange on credit vast chunks of landscape
wide segments of the bright prodigal river

ACKNOWLEDGEMENTS

Thanks are due to the editors and curators of the following publications and programmes in which some of these poems have appeared: *Icarus, Poetry Ireland Review, The Tangerine, The Stinging Fly, The Lifeboat, Bombinate, Unpredictapple, Amaryllis, RTÉ Culture, The Poetry Programme* and *Poetry JukeBox*.

A selection of these poems won the Patrick Kavanagh Award in 2018. Many thanks to Brian Lynch and the Patrick Kavanagh Society. Thanks also to Poetry Ireland for including me in their 2017 Introductions Series. Thanks to the Seamus Heaney Centre and Queen's University Belfast for a scholarship that allowed me to undertake an MA during which most of these poems were written. Many thanks to all my tutors and classmates and special thanks to Leontia Flynn who was the first reader of many of these poems. Thanks also to Ciaran Carson and everyone who attended his Friday workshops.

Special thanks to Luke Kennard and Conor O'Callaghan for their kind contributions to this pamphlet.

Thanks to Susannah Dickey, Fionn O'Shea, Rosa Jones, Seanín Hughes, Emily S. Cooper and Rosie O'Dowd for reading these poems in their various forms and offering advice and encouragement. Thanks to Richard O'Brien for his dedication and insight in editing this manuscript. Thanks also to Dawn Watson for her support and friendship. Thanks to my parents and my family for all their love. Thanks to Toby for everything.

ABOUT THE POET

Conor Cleary is from Tralee, Ireland, and lives in Glasgow. He has an MA in Poetry from Queen's University Belfast where he was the recipient of the 2016 Seamus Heaney Centre MA Award. In 2018, he was the winner of the Patrick Kavanagh Award.

His work has appeared in *Poetry Ireland Review, The Tangerine, Virginia Quarterly Review* and *The Stinging Fly*. This is his first poetry pamphlet.

ABOUT THE EMMA PRESS

The Emma Press is an independent publisher dedicated to producing beautiful, thought-provoking books. It was founded in 2012 by Emma Dai'an Wright in Winnersh, UK, and is now based in the Jewellery Quarter, Birmingham.

The Emma Press publishes poetry and fiction anthologies and pamphlets for adults and for children, with a growing list of translations.

The Emma Press has been shortlisted for the Michael Marks Award for Poetry Pamphlet Publishers in 2014, 2015, 2016 and 2018, winning in 2016.

theemmapress.com

www.ingramcontent.com/pod-product-compliance
Ingram Content Group UK Ltd.
Pitfield, Milton Keynes, MK11 3LW, UK
UKHW041014130425
457268UK00004B/82